Text by Alexander Fulton
Design by Philip Clucas MSIAD
Featuring the photography of
Neil Sutherland and Claude Poulet

CHARTWELL BOOKS
A division of Book Sales, Inc.
114 Northfield Avenue
Edison, NJ 08837 USA

CLB 4254
© 1995 CLB Publishing, Godalming, Surrey, U.K.
All rights reserved
Printed and bound in Singapore
ISBN 0-7858-0082-4

THE LITTLE BOOK OF
SCOTTISH
CLANS

BY
ALEXANDER FULTON

CHARTWELL
BOOKS, INC.

INTRODUCTION

The history of Scotland is a long one, full of the drama of war and rebellion, of emigration, clan loyalty, solidarity and achievement. Like all history, however, it is composed of countless individual family histories, each unique. Surnames are the point where history and individual clan histories intersect, marking individuality and kinship.

The Scottish clan or family tartan is of comparatively recent origin, but its genesis and development are inextricably linked with the colourful story of Scotland herself. Today, woven from the very fibre of Scotland's past, clan tartans transcend the nation's boundaries as the marks of kindred identities that span the world. What follows is an account of some of the most common clan surnames and their tartans, chosen purely because they *are* some of the most common, and therefore including some which are more usually seen as English or Irish. Any surname, borne by a Scottish person, whatever its origin, is a Scottish surname.

Facing page: autumn peace belies the drama
of the story of the Highlands.

ABERCROMBY

William of Abercromby in Fife did homage to King Edward I of England in 1296. His line became extinct in the seventeenth century and its place taken by that of Abercromby of Birkenbog, Banffshire.

Alexander Abercromby was grand falconer in Scotland to King Charles I. His eldest son, Alexander, was created 1st Baronet of Birkenbog by Charles I in 1636, but he was so active a Covenanter that, after the Battle of Auldearn in 1645, the Marquis of Montrose retaliated by billeting himself and some of his troops at Birkenbog.

Lieut-General Sir Ralph Abercromby (1734-1801), was born in Menstrie, near Tullibody. He took his troops to the Middle East, landing with them at Aboukir, and died of wounds received while personally leading them in an attack on the French forces at Alexandria. As a reward for her husband's bravery, his wife was created Baroness Abercromby of Aboukir and Tullibody.

ANDERSON (also MACANDREW)

The name means both 'son of Andrew' and 'servant of St Andrew', patron saint of Scotland. The Andersons of Dowhill go back at least to 1540. 'Little' John MacAndrew was a noted bowman, who in 1670 was on the receiving end of a cattle-rustling expedition in Badenoch by Lochaber men. The latter were hunted down and killed, bar one man who got home to tell the tale.

Professor John Anderson (1726-96) invented a field gun which he offered to the British Government, who refused it, so he presented the design to the French. He left instructions in his will for a university for working men to be founded in Glasgow. Though he left no money, his wish was followed. The Anderson's Institution is now Strathclyde University.

John Anderson (1882-1958), 1st Viscount Waverley, civil servant, politician, and statesman, was Governor of Bengal 1932-7, Home Secretary 1939-40, and Chancellor of the Exchequer 1943-5.

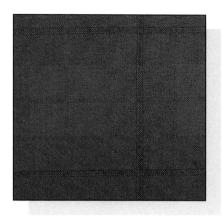

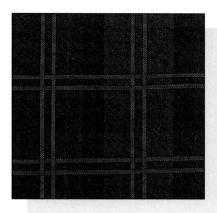

BARCLAY

The original Berkeleys came to England with William the Conqueror. One of them is said to have come to Scotland in 1069 and founded the branches of Ardrossan, Gartly, and Towie-Barclay.

In 1165 Sir Walter Barclay of Gartly became Chamberlain of Scotland under King William I, but the male Gartly line terminated in 1456. William Barclay (1547-1608), the lawyer and political philosopher, was most likely of the Collairnie branch.

Robert Barclay (1648-90), of the Urie branch, was a prominent Quaker, who was often imprisoned for his beliefs: in 1672 he paraded through Aberdeen clothed in sackcloth. Captain Robert Barclay-Allardyce of Urie (1779-1854) was a soldier and sportsman who, at Newmarket in 1809, walked 1,000 miles in 1,000 consecutive hours. Prince Barclay de Tolly (1761-1818), a descendant of the Tolly branch, was the Russian commander-in-chief during Napoleon's campaign of 1812.

BLAIR

Blair means 'moor' or 'field (of battle)', and the name derives from any of the places of that name.

Stephen de Blare witnessed a document to do with the monastery of Arbroath between 1204 and 1211, and Sir William de Blar was Seneschal of Fife in 1235.

John Blair was chaplain to Sir William Wallace (1274-1305), and wrote an account of the travels and adventures of that famous patriot and warrior, from which the poet known as Blind Harry claims to have taken material for his fifteenth century biographical romance in verse, *Schir William Wallace*. The Blairs of Blair are an old Renfrewshire family, and an ancient lineage is also claimed for the Blairs of Balthayock, Perthshire. In 1770 James Hunter (1741-87), an Edinburgh banker, married Jean Blair (*d.* 1817), daughter and heiress of John Blair of Dunksey. Hunter assumed the name of Hunter Blair in 1777, and was created a baronet in 1786.

BOYD

The first recorded Boyd is Sir Robert Boyd, so called because his hair was fair (Gaelic *buidhe*). Sir Robert Boyd was a commander for King Robert I (the Bruce) at the Battle of Bannockburn in 1314, for which he was granted land, including Kilmarnock and Kilbride. Robert Boyd of Kilmarnock (*d*. 1482) was made Lord Boyd by King James II, and in 1468 he negotiated the marriage between King James III and the daughter of the King of Norway, whereby Orkney and the Shetland Isles were ceded to Scotland. William Boyd (*d*. 1692) was made Earl of Kilmarnock at the Restoration of Charles II. The Boyds of Penkill, Pitcon and Trochrig are descended from Alexander Boyd, Chamberlain of Kilmarnock 1488-1504. Alan Tindale Lennox-Boyd (*b*. 1904) of Merton-in-Penninghame, Wigtownshire, was created Viscount Boyd of Merton in 1960, his descent being from Rev. William Boyd (1658-1741), Minister of Dalry, Kircudbrightshire.

BRODIE

There was a Malcolm, Thane of Brodie, at the time of King Alexander III in the thirteenth century, and his son Michael was granted lands by King Robert I (the Bruce) in 1311. The family goes back much farther than this, however, and is believed to be of ancient Pictish stock.

Alexander Brodie of Brodie (1617-80) was a Covenanter, who in 1640 led the assault on Elgin Cathedral which destroyed two valuable paintings and mutilated the interior carvings, as being inappropriate for a place of worship. In the wars that followed, Brodie House was razed and the family records destroyed. Brodie himself was appointed a judge of the Court of Session in 1649, but at the restoration of the monarchy in 1660 he was replaced and fined £4,000 Scots, despite having done his best to avoid carrying out any orders of Cromwell, Lord Protector of England.

BRUCE

Robert de Brus came to England with William the Conqueror in 1066. His son, Robert, was granted the lands of Annandale by King David I in 1124. The fifth Robert de Brus (or Bruce) married Isabella, great-granddaughter of David I, and their son, Robert de Bruce (1210-95), known as the 'Competitor', claimed the throne of Scotland on the death of Alexander III's little granddaughter, Margaret, 'Maid of Norway'. King Edward I of England ruled in favour of John Balliol, on whose abdication in 1306 the eighth Robert de Bruce, Robert I (the Bruce), seized the throne, and in a glorious but desperately fought reign defeated the English at Bannockburn in 1314. When he died in 1329 he had secured immortality for himself and, for a time, independence for Scotland. The family succession continued with King Robert II, son of the Bruce's daughter Marjorie, who married Walter the Steward, thus inaugurating the House of Stewart.

BURNS, BURNES, BURNESS

The name probably derives from places in Scotland with a similar spelling or sound. Robert Burnes, a farmer in Kincardineshire, had three sons. The youngest, William (1721-84), a tenant farmer, died bankrupt. *His* elder son, Robert (1759-96), dropped the 'e' from his name, and overcame the handicap of an indigent upbringing to become the most famous of all Scottish poets. He composed technically brilliant love songs, satires and nature poems, as well as *Tam o' Shanter*, his version of a scary folk tale which is recited all over the world today on his birthday. The talents of the family did not stop with him. William Burnes's eldest brother, James, was great-grandfather of James Burnes (1801-62), Physician-General of Bombay, and Sir Alexander Burnes (1805-41) who was the first westerner to follow the course of the River Indus, and was assassinated in Kabul, having done his best to avert interference in Afghanistan by both India and Russia.

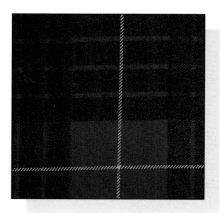

CAMERON

The Camerons' name is supposed to come from the Gaelic *cam-shron* (crooked nose), said to have been a feature of an early chief. The first recorded chief, Donald Dubh, fought with the Mackintoshes in the Battle of Harlaw in 1411, but by 1430 the Camerons and the Mackintoshes were feuding over a land dispute, and remained so for two centuries.

The 13th Chief took the suffix 'Lochiel', and his family has held the chiefship of Clan Cameron ever since. Sir Ewen Cameron of Lochiel (1629-1719), the 17th Chief, is attributed with killing the last wolf in Scotland, and with biting out the throat of an officer in an attack on a government fortress.

In 1793 Major Allan Cameron of Erracht (1753-1828) raised the Camerons' own regiment, the 79th Highlanders, which became the Queen's Own Cameron Highlanders in 1873, and since 1961, when it was merged with the Seaforths, has been the Queen's Own Highlanders.

CAMPBELL

The surname Campbell, most probably derived from the Gaelic *cam-beul* (twisted mouth), is one of the oldest in the Highlands, and a crown charter of 1368 acknowledges Duncan MacDuihbne as founder of the Campbells, who were established as lords of Loch Awe. The founder of the Argyll line was *Cailean Mór* (*d.* 1294), whose descendant, Colin Campbell (*d.* 1493), 1st Earl of Argyll, married Isabel Stewart of Lorne. To this day the eldest son of the family has borne the title of Marquis of Lorne.

Sir John Campbell (1635-1716), 11th Laird of Glenorchy, was created Earl of Breadalbane in 1681. Described as being 'cunning as a fox, wise as a serpent, and supple as an eel … [who] knew neither honour nor religion but where they are mixed with interest', he was involved in the scheming which resulted in the Massacre of Glencoe, but no evidence of his guilt could be produced.

The founder of the Cawdor branch, another Sir John Campbell (*d*. 1546), obtained his lands through his wife Muriel (1495-1573). An orphan who had inherited her father's title of Thane of Cawdor, she was kidnapped in 1499 by Campbell's father, Archibald (*d*. 1513), 2nd Earl of Argyll, and married to his son in 1510. The Campbells of Loudoun are descended from Sir Duncan Campbell, second son of the first *MacCailean Mór*, who married a Crauford of Loudoun. The Earldom of Loudoun, created for John Campbell (1598-1663), politician, has since the eighteenth century descended through the female line.

Eilean Donan Castle, Ross and Cromarty

CARMICHAEL

Robert de Caramicely is mentioned in 1226, the name probably deriving from lands in Lanarkshire which were granted to Sir James Douglas in 1321, and by his nephew to Sir John Carmichael between 1374 and 1384.

Sir James Carmichael (1579-1672) was created Lord Carmichael by King Charles I in 1647, and his grandson, John (1672-1710), who was Secretary of State for Scotland 1696-1707 and Chancellor of Glasgow University, was made Earl of Hyndford in 1701. Richard Carmichael of Carmichael (*b.* 1948), the present chief, has done a great deal to revitalise the Carmichael heritage.

CARNEGIE

In 1358 King David II confirmed that the owner of the lands of Carnegie was John of Carnegie, direct descendant of Jocelyn de Ballinhard, who first held them in 1203. Sir David Carnegie of Kinnaird (1575-1628), was made Earl of Southesk in 1633, when King Charles I came north for his Scottish coronation. The youngest of his six daughters, Magdalen (*d.* 1648), married the illustrious Marquis of Montrose when he was only seventeen. Southesk's brother, John Carnegie of Ethie (1579-1667), was made Earl of Ethie in 1647, the title being changed to Northesk in 1666. William, 7th Earl of Northesk (1758-1831), was third in command under Nelson of the British fleet at the Battle of Trafalgar in 1805.

The philanthropist Andrew Carnegie (1835-1918) was the son of a Dunfermline weaver who emigrated to the USA in 1848. He retired to Skibo Castle in Sutherland in 1901, and spent the rest of his life distributing the vast fortune he had made.

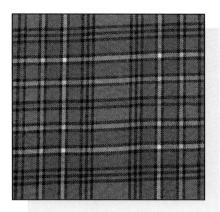

COCKBURN

The lands of Cockburn were in Berwickshire, and the name is quite widely recorded in the thirteenth century.

Sir Alexander Cockburn fell at the Battle of Bannockburn in 1314, and his grandson, Alexander Cockburn, was Keeper of the Great Seal 1389-96. In 1595 Sir William Cockburn was granted the Barony of Langton, Berwickshire, and his descendant, Sir Alexander Cockburn (1802-80), was Lord Chief Justice of England. Adam Cockburn of Ormiston (1656-1735), Lord Justice Clerk and one of the members of the commission which enquired into the Massacre of Glencoe, was created Lord Ormiston. Henry Cockburn (1779-1854), son of a sheriff of Midlothian, judge and man of letters, was made Lord Cockburn in 1834.

CRAWFORD

The Crawfords, Crawfurds, or Craufurds get their name from the Barony of Crawford in Lanarkshire. Sir John Crawfurd (*d.* 1248) had two daughters. From the younger are descended the earls of Crawford. Sir Archibald Crawford, Sheriff of Ayr, was treacherously murdered by the English at a banquet in his home town in 1297. His sister Margaret married Sir Malcolm Wallace of Elderslie, and their son Sir William Wallace (1274-1305) was the famous Scottish patriot and warrior.

In 1781 a baronetcy was conferred on Alexander Craufurd of Kilbirnie, who had three distinguished sons: Sir James Craufurd, British Ambassador in Hamburg 1798-1803; Lieut-General Sir Charles Gregan-Craufurd (1761-1821), who served with great daring in the Netherlands in 1794; and Major-General Robert Craufurd (1764-1812), commander of the Light Brigade in the Peninsular War.

CUNNINGHAM

Wernibald of Cunningham, Ayrshire, is said to have been granted the property of Kilmaurs in about 1140, and a Harvey Cunningham of Kilmaurs was among those who helped King Alexander III repel a Norse sea-force at the Battle of Largs in 1263.

Sir Alexander Cunningham of Kilmaurs (*d.* 1488) was made Lord Kilmaurs in about 1450, and Earl of Glencairn in 1488, for his part in opposing the lords who rebelled against King James III, but he was killed a fortnight later in the Battle of Sauchiburn. The branches of Auchinharvie, Craigends, and Robertland derive from his second son. Alexander Cunningham (*d.* 1574), 5th Earl of Glencairn, was a Protestant zealot who did his utmost to upset the order of things during the reign of Mary, Queen of Scots. James Cunningham (1749-91), 14th Earl, was the friend and patron of Robert Burns, and after his death and that of his brother, the earldom became dormant.

DOUGLAS

No single family, apart from the Stewarts, has contributed so much to the course of Scottish history as that of Douglas. William de Douglas lived at the end of the twelfth century. His younger son Andrew was ancestor of the earls of Morton, of whom James Douglas (1525-81), 4th Earl by virtue of his marriage to his predecessor's daughter, was the infamous Regent Morton during the boyhood of King James VI, who finally had him beheaded for his part in the murder of Lord Darnley fourteen years earlier. The elder son of William, Sir William Douglas, was father of 'Good Sir James' (1286-1330), who was the right hand man of King Robert I (the Bruce) at the Battle of Bannockburn in 1314 and after it. He was called the Black Douglas from his complexion, a nickname which became attached to his line. Sir James's nephew William became 1st Earl of Douglas in 1358 and had an affair with Margaret, widow of his wife's brother, and the

A parade of pipers at the Braemar Gathering, which is held each September in the resort's Princess Royal Park.

outcome was George (1380-1403), who in 1389 was granted the title of Earl of Angus and became known as the Red Douglas. The Black Douglases went through some harrowing times. The young but powerful 6th Earl (1423-40) was lured to Edinburgh Castle, seized and tried in the presence of the boy King James II, and then beheaded. James II himself stabbed to death the 8th Earl (1425-50) in Stirling Castle. The earldom was forfeited by the 9th Earl (1426-88) and passed to the Red Douglases. Archibald (1489-1557), 6th Earl, married Margaret Tudor (1489-1541), widow of King James IV, and was thus the grandfather of Lord Darnley and great-grandfather of King James VI.

DRUMMOND

The first recorded Drummond is Sir Malcolm de Drummond, who disabled the English cavalry at the Battle of Bannockburn in 1314 by spreading caltrops, ingenious spiked objects, in their way. His granddaughter Margaret married King David II in 1362, while his great granddaughter Annabella (*d.* 1401) was mother of King James I. Sir John Drummond was made Lord Drummond in 1488. His daughter Margaret was engaged to King James IV but was poisoned just before he married Margaret Tudor, daughter of King Henry VII of England. The 4th Lord Drummond was created Earl of Perth in 1605, and in 1609 his uncle was made Lord Maderty, the 4th Lord Maderty becoming Viscount Strathallan in 1686. As active Jacobites, the 3rd Duke was wounded and the 4th Viscount killed at the Battle of Culloden in 1746, after which both families had their estates forfeited. The chiefship of the clan was restored to Scotland only in 1902.

DUNBAR

The stark remains of Dunbar Castle, off the coast of East Lothian, tell many stories. The 1st Earl of Dunbar, nephew of King Duncan I, was granted the lands by King Malcolm III in 1072. Patrick (1285-1368), 9th Earl, married Agnes (1312-69), known as 'Black Agnes'. She was the daughter of the 1st Earl of Moray and is celebrated for her defence of the castle against the English for five months in 1338. She inherited the earldom of Moray, that and the earldom of Dunbar ultimately devolving on the sons of her sister Isobel. This connection between Dunbar and Moray resulted in the Dunbar family being officially recognised as a Highland clan in 1579. James Dunbar (*d.* 1430), 4th and last Earl of Moray of that line, had a son, Sir Alexander Dunbar of Westfield (*d.* 1498). He was appointed the first hereditary Sheriff of Moray, and from him descended the Dunbars of Mochrum, who were created baronets in 1694 and hold the chiefship of the clan.

DUNCAN

The Duncans, like the Robertsons, are descended from the ancient earls of Atholl, and took their name from the chief, *Donnachadh Reamar* (Duncan the Fat), who led them at the Battle of Bannockburn in 1314.

Adam Duncan of Lundie (1731-1804) was the second son of a royalist provost of Dundee, and at six feet four inches was of enormous height for his time. He joined the Royal Navy in 1746, and in 1795 was appointed to command the North Sea fleet. He successfully blockaded the Dutch coastline for two years, in spite of his ships being reduced by mutiny, and in 1779 scored a brilliant tactical victory at Camperdown. He was created Baron Duncan of Lundie and Viscount Duncan of Camperdown in 1800.

DUNLOP

The lands of Dunlop are in Ayrshire, and the name is first recorded in 1260. James Dunlop possessed the estate at the beginning of the fifteenth century, but his descendant, John Dunlop, for his support of the Covenanters, was forced to hand over a large part of it to Lord Dundonald, though it was returned to his grandson later. Francis Dunlop (*d*. 1748) fought as a colonel against the Jacobites in 1715, his son marrying Frances Anne Wallace (1730-1815), the friend and patron of Robert Burns (1759-96). Their son, General James Dunlop (*d*. 1832), fought in the Duke of Wellington's army in 1811. John Boyd Dunlop (1840-1921), inventor of the pneumatic tyre, was born in Dreghorn, Ayrshire. Thomas Dunlop (1855-1938), Glasgow shipowner and merchant, was made a baronet in 1916.

ELLIOT(T)

The Elliots, with the Armstrongs, were the most troublesome of the great Border families in the Middle Ages, the Redheugh branch being regarded as the most influential of them. Robert Elwold (or Elliot) of Redheugh fell at the Battle of Flodden in 1513, and from his third son came the Elliots of Arkleton. The Stobs branch stems from 1584, and to it descended the Redheugh lands. Gilbert Elliot of Stobs (1651-1718), known as 'Gibbie with the Golden Garters', was convicted of high treason in 1685 for plotting against the Catholic Duke of York, but was pardoned, and after the accession of William of Orange in 1689 he was knighted, appointed Clerk to the Privy Council, made a judge, and created Lord Minto. His son Gilbert (1693-1766), Lord Justice Clerk of Scotland, was the father of the talented Jean Elliot of Minto (1727-1805), author of the best version of all of the traditional song *The Flowers of the Forest*.

ERSKINE

Henry of Erskine held the Barony of Erskine, Renfrewshire, in the reign of King Alexander II in the thirteenth century. Sir Robert of Erskine (*d.* 1385), Great Chamberlain of Scotland 1350-7, whose prompt action in 1371 against the claim of the Douglas family saved the throne for King Robert II, was granted a charter for the Barony of Dun in 1376. His son Thomas married the heiress to the earldom of Mar, and their younger son founded the branch of Dun. The elder son, Robert, assumed the title of Earl of Mar, but was stripped of it on a technicality in 1457, and created Lord Erskine in 1467. Robert, 4th Lord Erskine, and many Erskines of Dun, fell at the Battle of Flodden in 1513. His grandson John (*d.* 1572), 6th Lord, Regent of Scotland during the sojourn in France of Mary, Queen of Scots (he later carried her son, the baby King James VI, at his coronation in 1567), was restored by her to the earldom of Mar in 1565.

FERGUS(S)ON

The Fergussons (the spelling of the name with a single 's' is not known before the eighteenth century) are a widely spread clan, major families of which were established in various parts of Scotland before the sixteenth century. The Fergussons of Craigdarroch in the southwest probably came from Fergus, Prince of Galloway, who was a prominent figure in the twelfth century and founded the Abbey of Dundrennan. The Fergussons of Kilkerran, Ayrshire, may be descended from 'John, son of Fergus', who witnessed a document after the Battle of Bannockburn in 1314. During the eighteenth century the head of the Kilkerran branch came to be regarded as chief of the clan. The Fergussons of Atholl have a forebear in 'Adam, son of Fergus', who held lands in Perthshire in the second half of the thirteenth century. An earlier ancestor is claimed for all of them, however, Fergus *Mór mac Erc*, a very early, and shadowy, king of the Scots in Argyll.

FORBES

Forbes is an ancient Aberdeenshire parish. The founder of the clan, one Oconochar, slew a bear, which was occupying the Braes o' Forbes, and took up occupation there. The tenure was confirmed by a charter of 1271. Sir John Forbes (*d.* 1406), 'John of the Black Lip', had four sons from whom branches of the clan are descended.

The Forbeses were great builders of castles, notably Corse Castle, built in 1581 by William Forbes, who was so frustrated by burglars that he vowed, 'I will build me such a house as thieves will need to knock at ere they enter'. The result, a tower-house, was later the home of his eldest son, Patrick (1564-1635), Bishop of Aberdeen. Only a few miles away, still standing is romantic Craigievar Castle, completed in 1626 by the Bishop's brother, William, known as 'Danzig Willie', for his activities as a merchant in the Baltic.

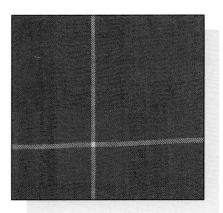

FRASER

The first known Fraser in Scotland was Simon Fraser, who in about 1160 donated the church of Keith to Kelso Abbey. The name came from the lordship of La Fraselière in Anjou, and a descendant of Simon Fraser, Sir Gilbert Fraser, established the main line of the family in about 1250 at Touch-Fraser, Stirlingshire. His direct descendant, Alexander Fraser (*d.* 1332), was knighted by King Robert I (the Bruce) before the Battle of Bannockburn in 1314. He married the Bruce's sister, Lady Mary and was later Chamberlain of Scotland. Their grandson gained the lands of Philorth in Buchan by his marriage in 1375.

The Frasers of Lovat are descended from Sir Alexander Fraser (1537-1623), 8th Laird of Philorth's younger brother, Simon, who also fought at Bannockburn, and each chief of Clan Fraser of Lovat is known as *MacShimi* (son of Simon).

GALBRAITH

The Galbraiths are known in Gaelic as *Clann o'Bhreatannaich*, 'the British clan', and its earliest members were Britons from north Wales who settled in Strathclyde, which was a separate kingdom until 1018. The first known chief is Gilchrist *Bretnach*, while James, 19th Chief, is the last of the direct line of whom there is any trace. He was the grandson of Robert Galbraith of Culcreuch, 17th Chief, who died in Ireland in about 1640, a fugitive from justice, having given up all his lands to settle his debts. In 1592 Robert was one of those given a commission to harry the unfortunate MacGregors, but instead used his powers of 'fire and sword' to make life uncomfortable for Sir Aulay Macaulay (*d.* 1617), chief of the Macaulays, who had married his widowed mother against his wishes.

Thomas Galbraith (1891-1985), created 1st Lord Strathclyde in 1955, was descended from William Galbraith of Blackhouse (1678-1757), Stirlingshire.

GORDON

The name comes from the parish of Gordon in Berwickshire, and Sir Adam of Gordon (*d.* 1333) was granted Strathbogie in Aberdeenshire by King Robert I (the Bruce), in recognition of his services in reconciling the Bruce with the Pope and towards securing peace with England. His great-great-granddaughter, heiress to the family estates, married Alexander Seton of Seton, who took the name of Gordon, and their son Alexander was created Earl of Huntly in 1449.

The Gordons wielded enormous power during the sixteenth and early seventeenth centuries, to the extent that their chief was known as 'Cock of the North'. The 6th Earl was made Marquis in 1599, but the 2nd Marquis was beheaded in 1649 by the Scottish Parliament for his loyalty to King Charles I, going to the block with the words, 'You may take my head from my shoulders, but not my heart from my king.'

GUTHRIE

The family held the Barony of Guthrie, Forfar, in the fourteenth century, but earlier than this, in 1299, Squire Guthrie was sent to France by the northern lords to bring back Sir William Wallace (1274-1305) to help his country against the English.

Sir David Guthrie, armour-bearer to King James III and Lord Treasurer of Scotland 1461-7, had a charter in 1468 to build a tower and castle on the Guthrie lands.

An old rhyme, printed in 1841 in *Popular Rhymes of Scotland*, lists the branches of this 'respectable old Forfarshire family': 'Guthrie o' Guthrie/Guthrie o' Gaiggie/Guthrie o' Taybank/An' Guthrie o' Craigie.'

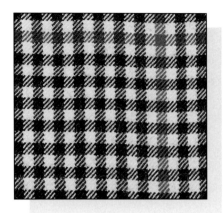

HAIG

Peter de Haga, 1st Laird of Bemersyde, Roxburghshire, witnessed several charters made to the monks of Melrose in the twelfth century. The 27th Laird, Sophia Haig, died unmarried in 1878, and Bemersyde passed to Lieut-Colonel Arthur Haig (1840-1925), descended from a younger son of the 17th Laird. He sold it in 1921 so that it could be presented by the nation, for his services during World War I, to Field-Marshal Sir Douglas, 1st Earl Haig (1861-1928), another descendant of the 17th Laird, who thus became 29th Laird.

Facing page: correct outdoor wear: a Highland bonnet complete with a clansman's badge, in this instance bearing the cheerful motto 'Dum spiro spero', 'While I breathe, I hope'.

HAMILTON

Walter FitzGilbert, son of Gilbert of Hamilton, was given the Barony of Cadzow by King Robert I (the Bruce), his descendant, James Hamilton (*d.* 1479), 6th Laird, being made Lord Hamilton in 1445. Lord Hamilton's son by his second wife, Mary, was created Earl of Arran in 1503, and from him descended the marquises of Hamilton (Dukes from 1643) and the earls of Abercorn. Mary was a daughter of King James II and through that marriage the Hamiltons were for much of the sixteenth century heirs presumptive to the throne.

Sir Thomas Hamilton (1563-1637), descended from a minor branch of the family, was Lord President of the Court of Session and Keeper of the Privy Seal. He was created Lord Binning in 1613, and in 1619 Earl of Melrose, which he successfully petitioned to be changed to Haddington in 1626.

HAY

William de Hay, of Norman descent, was joint hereditary cupbearer both to King Malcolm IV and King William I (the Lion). Between 1178 and 1182 he received from King William the Barony of Erroll. Sir Gilbert Hay, 5th Laird and Clan Chief, was made hereditary Constable of Scotland by King Robert I (the Bruce) and given Slains Castle, Buchan, which was destroyed by King James VI in 1595. The 4th High Constable married a daughter of King Robert II, and the Hays of Delgaty are descended from their second son. The elder son was grandfather of William, made Earl of Erroll in 1452. William, 4th Earl, was killed at the Battle of Flodden in 1513, along with 87 other Hays. The family also engendered the marquises of Tweeddale (through the Yester branch) and the earls of Kinnoull (through the Megginch and Kinfauns branch), but the office of chief constable and, presently, the chiefship of the clan are vested in the earls of Erroll.

HENDERSON (or MACKENDRICK)

The Highland Hendersons claim to be descended from Eanruig Mór (Big Henry), son of Nechtan, King of the Picts in 710. A further tradition has it that the chiefship of the Hendersons of Glencoe passed through an heiress to her son, *Iain Fruoch* (Heather John), progenitor of the unfortunate McIans of Glencoe.

Other Hendersons in Caithness are descendants of Hendry, son of 'Crowner George' Gunn. Alexander Henderson (1583-1646), the Covenanter and Presbyterian divine who drafted the Solemn League and Covenant in 1643, was a Henderson of Fordell, with descent from James Henderson, 1st Laird of Fordell, Lord Advocate in 1494.

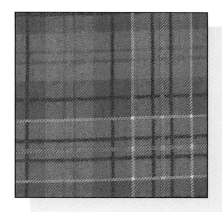

HEPBURN

Hepburns are first heard of in Northumberland, and Adam de Hibburne was granted Hailes, in East Lothian, among other lands by the Earl of March, 'for good and faithful service', which appears to have included saving his life from an attack by a wild horse.

Patrick de Hepburn of Hailes, who, with his father, fought at the Battle of Otterburn in 1388, was twice married. His great-grandson by his first wife was made Earl of Bothwell in 1488. James Hepburn (1536-78), 4th Earl of Bothwell, was the third husband of Mary, Queen of Scots. He died insane, a prisoner in Denmark, having forfeited all his titles and without legitimate issue.

From Patrick of Hailes by his second wife descended the Hepburns of Smeaton Hepburn, the estate passing to Sir George Buchan-Hepburn (1738-1819).

HUNTER OF HUNTERSTON

The name derives from the hunt, and therefore it occurs widely at an early stage. The Hunters of Hunterston appear to have held the lands in Ayrshire in the early part of the thirteenth century, and obtained a charter for them in 1375.

William Hunter (1718-1783), the anatomist, whose acquisitions of paintings, artefacts, fossils, coins, and anatomical and pathological specimens are still the basis of the collections at the Hunterian Museum, Glasgow University, and his brother John (1728-93), the surgeon, were descended from a younger son of Patrick Hunter, great-grandson of Mungo, or Quentegern, Hunter of Hunterston, who fell at the Battle of Pinkie in 1547.

Neil Kennedy-Cochran-Patrick (b. 1926) was officially recognised by the Lyon Court in 1969 in the name of Hunter of Hunterston as being 29th Laird of Hunterston and Chief of Clan Hunter.

IRVINE

Irwins held lands in Dumfriesshire at the beginning of the thirteenth century. A member of that family, William de Irwin, was armour-bearer to King Robert I (the Bruce), who granted him the forest of Drum, Aberdeenshire, in 1324. From him descended the Irvines of Drum, the principal family of that name. Sir Alexander Irvine of Drum (*d.* 1658) was a confirmed royalist to whom King Charles I gave the earldom of Aberdeen, but the outbreak of the Civil War prevented him from formally accepting it. The offer was renewed to his son by King Charles II after the Restoration of the Monarchy in 1660, but was refused.

The art of throwing the hammer at the annual Braemar Gathering: only the strong need apply!

JOHNSTON(E)

This Border clan, which from 1585 to 1623 waged war against the Maxwells, probably originated with Sir Gilbert de Johnstoun in about 1200. At various times the chiefship has been vested in the line of Lord Johnstone (created 1633), whose son was made Earl of Annandale and Hartfell (1661), and his great-grandson Marquis of Annandale (1701). The Johnstons of Westerhall are descended from an early offshoot of the main stem, and the 3rd Baronet was made Lord Derwent in 1881.

An Aberdeenshire line claims descent from Steven de Johnston, a fourteenth-century scholar, whose grandson founded the branch of Caskieben, and whose family was granted a Nova Scotia baronetcy in 1626. Sir John Johnston, 3rd Baronet, was hanged in 1690 for being present at the wedding of Capt. the Hon. James Campbell and Mary Wharton, an heiress whom Campbell was said to have abducted.

KEITH

The story of the Keiths is the progress of the marischals of Scotland, hereditary keepers of the royal horses. After the Battle of Worcester was lost by Charles I, William (1617-71), 7th Earl Marischal, who was also Warden of the Regalia of Scotland, sent the crown jewels to his castle on the coast at Dunnottar for safety. The English knew they were there, and for eight months laid siege to the castle, which was finally stormed after ten solid days of bombardment by cannon. The regalia, however, had already been lowered over the battlements to the shore, where the maid from the nearby manse of Kinneff, who was often seen collecting seaweed, put them into her basket and took them away. Eight years later, at the Restoration of Charles II, the items were produced, and for his part in the operation, the 8th Earl Marischal, brother of the 7th Earl, was created Earl Kintore, with the Latin motto, *Quae amissa salva* (Save what has been lost).

KENNEDY

The Kennedys emerged in Ayrshire. In the fourteenth century John Kennedy of Dunure, having acquired Cassilis by his first marriage, married as his second wife Mary of Carrick, with whom came to him the right to be chief of the men of Carrick. Their grandson, Sir James Kennedy of Dunure (*d.* 1409) was second husband of Mary Stewart, daughter of Robert III. Of their three sons, James (1408-65), was Bishop of St Andrews and adviser to King James II, and Gilbert (1406-80) was made Lord Kennedy in 1457. The 3rd Lord was created Earl of Cassilis in 1509 and died in the Battle of Flodden in 1513. The 3rd Earl was one of the members of the commission for the marriage of Mary, Queen of Scots, to the Dauphin of France, who were poisoned in 1558.

The earldom of Cassilis passed to the Kennedys of Culzean in 1759. Culzean Castle, built round an ancient tower of the Kennedys, dates from 1777.

KERR

The first recorded Kerr (or Ker or Carr) is John Ker of Swinhope, near Peebles, in the twelfth century. The branches of Cessford and Ferniehurst are said to have descended from two brothers who lived in about 1330. There was the greatest rivalry between them, sometimes bloody. The Cessford Kerrs received their grant of land in 1467, and built a castle on it, while a younger son got by marriage the castle of Ferniehurst, a few miles away.

For some years the Warden of the Middle March was alternately a Cessford and a Ferniehurst. Andrew Kerr of Ferniehurst was made Lord Jedburgh in 1662, the title devolving on the marquises of Lothian, who were descended from Mark Kerr, commendator (licensee) of Newbattle Abbey in 1547.

Sir Robert Kerr of Cessford (*d.* 1650) was made Earl of Roxburghe in 1616. John Ker (*d.* 1741), 5th Earl, was created 1st Duke of Roxburghe in 1707 for furthering the union of the two parliaments.

LAUDER

The name comes from Lauder in Berwickshire, and in the thirteenth century the Lauders owned Bass Rock in the Firth of Forth.

John Lauder (*d*. 1692), an Edinburgh merchant, who received the Barony of Fountainhall in 1681, was created a baronet in 1690. Sir John Lauder (*d*. 1722), 2nd Baronet, a judge of the Court of Session, was made Lord Fountainhall in 1689. The 5th Baronet married his cousin Isobel (*d*. 1758), heiress of William Dick of Grange. The family name was changed to Dick-Lauder in the time of the 7th Baronet, Sir Thomas Dick-Lauder (1784-1848), author and antiquary, whom the Sobieski Stuart brothers enlisted as a supporter of the authenticity of their tartan theories and creations.

Sir Harry Lauder (1870-1950), the famous entertainer, was born in Musselburgh.

LENNOX

The name of the district of Lennox comes from the Gaelic for the Vale of Leven, where the Celtic earls of Lennox held sway from the twelfth to the fifteenth centuries. Sir John Stewart of Darnley (*d*. 1495) was created 1st Earl of Lennox of the new line by King James III in 1473, and Henry Stuart (1545-67), Lord Darnley, eldest son of the 4th Earl of Lennox, was the second husband of Mary, Queen of Scots, and father of King James VI, who promoted the 8th Earl to be Duke of Lennox in 1581.

On the death of the 6th Duke, who was drowned at Elsinore in 1672, the title devolved on King Charles II, who passed it on to Charles (1672-1723), his illegitimate son by his mistress, the Duchess of Portsmouth. The infant Charles, who was already 1st Duke of Richmond (Yorkshire), thus in 1675 became also Duke of Lennox and Earl of Darnley.

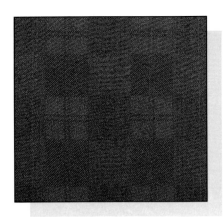

LESLIE

Bertolf, a Hungarian noble, chamberlain to Margaret (St Margaret, wife of King Malcolm III), sister of Edgar the Atheling, came with them to Scotland in 1070, and claimed vacant lands in Aberdeenshire, which were confirmed as the lands of Leslie to his son, Malcolm.

George Leslie of Ballinbreich, a descendant of the 6th Laird of Leslie, was made 1st Earl of Rothes by King James II. John (1630-81), 7th Earl, carried the sword of state at the Scottish coronation of King Charles II in 1651. At the Battle of Worcester that same year, he led a regiment of horse in the King's army. Rothes was appointed Lord Chancellor in 1670, and made Duke of Rothes, Marquis of Ballenbreich, and Earl Leslie in 1680. He had no sons. His daughter Margaret married Charles Hamilton, 5th Earl of Haddington: their elder son inherited from his mother the earldom of Rothes, while the younger became 6th Earl of Haddington.

LINDSAY

The first recorded Lindsay in Scotland, Sir Walter, arrived in the twelfth century from England, where his Norman forebears had held lands since the Norman Conquest.

In about 1346 Sir David Lindsay of Crawford, in Lanarkshire, acquired Glenesk, in Angus, by marriage. His younger son was Sir William Lindsay of the Byres, Haddington. The elder was Alexander Lindsay of Glenesk, whose son Sir David Lindsay (1365-1407) inherited from a cousin the Barony of Crawford and in 1398 was made Earl of Crawford.

David Lindsay's younger son, John Lindsay of Balcarres, Fife, was father of David Lindsay, an alchemist and patron of literature, who was made Earl of Balcarres and hereditary Keeper of Edinburgh Castle by King Charles II in 1651. The two earldoms came together in 1808.

LIVINGSTON(E)

Livingston, near Linlithgow, was the 'toun' or estate of a twelfth-century Saxon called Living, whose descendants took the name. By collecting for themselves offices of state (and with them castles), the family became enormously powerful in the fifteenth century, until the young King James II decided in 1449 that he had had enough of them, whereupon he imprisoned his former guardian, Sir Alexander Livingstone of Callander (*d.* 1450), and others of his family, and executed two of his sons. The Livingstones of Barncloich, Bonton, Kinnaird, and Westquarter descended from Sir Alexander's brothers. The Livingstones from Argyll and the Hebrides claim descent from a physician to the Lord of the Isles, the name *Mac-an-leigh* (son of the physician) becoming in English Livingston. A very distant and, by birth, humble descendant was Dr David Livingstone (1813-73), the explorer of Africa and missionary.

MacAULAY

There are two distinct families, or branches, of the name. The MacAulays of Ardincaple, Dumbartonshire, were one of the clans of MacAlpine, and the name of MacAulay appears in the Ragman Roll of 1296, by which signatories acknowledged their homage to King Edward I of England. The lands of Ardincaple were sold to the 4th Duke of Argyll in 1767.

The MacAulays of Lewis claim descent from Aula, or Olaf the Black, a thirteenth-century king of the Isles. From this family, and from a line of Calvinist ministers, descended Thomas Babington Macaulay (1800-59), 1st Lord Macaulay, poet, critic, and the first historian to popularise the subject.

MacBETH

The presumed ancestor of the clan is Macbeth (1005-1057), Mormaer (High Steward) of Moray, whose mother was said to have been a daughter of King Kenneth II. He married, as her second husband, Gruoch, daughter of a son of King Kenneth III. Under the ancient law of the Scots he had as much claim to the throne of Scotland as King Duncan I, against whom he rebelled, and whom he defeated and killed in battle in 1040. He was proclaimed king, and Scotland prospered during his reign.

In 1369 King David II granted a charter for lands in Angus to a family of Macbeths, who were descended from the major Fife family of Bethune. A further family, called *MacBeatha*, practised as physicians to the lords of the Isles at much the same time as a family of Bethunes were notable physicians in Skye. This has caused confusion as in the Highlands the names Macbeth, Bethune, and Beaton were often interchangeable.

MacDONALD

Somerled (*d.* 1164), ruler of the Isles, had three sons, who divided up his territory between them. The second son, Reginald (*d.* 1207), also had three sons, of whom Donald (*d.* 1289) gave his name to the clan. Donald's grandson, John (*d.* 1386), took the formal title of Lord of the Isles in 1354. He also married, as his second wife, Margaret, one of the thirteen children of King Robert II's first marriage. Their son, Donald (*d.* 1423), 2nd Lord of the Isles, became through his wife, Mary Leslie, uncle by marriage of Euphemia, who had inherited the earldom of Ross from her mother in 1402 but had inconveniently become a nun, and thus was legally counted as dead. Donald wanted the earldom of Ross, and in 1411 decided to invade the Lowlands as a means of persuading the Regency (King James I being in captivity in England) to let him have it. His son, Alexander (*d.* 1449), 3rd Lord of the Isles, did succeed to the earldom of Ross and his youngest son, Hugh (*d.* 1498), got as his inheritance the region of Sleat in Skye, and is the founder of the MacDonalds of Sleat.

The MacDonalds of Clanranald are descended from Ranald, younger son of the first marriage of John, 1st Lord of the Isles. Ranald received the northern islands and other lands in 1373 and was the ancestor of the branches of MacDonalds of Knoidart, Moidart, and Morar. The MacDonalds of Clanranald, under their sixteen-year-old chief, were among the first of the clans to rally to Viscount Dundee at Lochaber in 1689, and were in continuous support of Bonnie Prince Charlie. Flora MacDonald (1722-1790), chief heroine of the escape, was of Clanranald through her father's line.

Highland tranquility

MacDUFF

Constantine, Earl of Fife, who died in about 1129, is said to have been of the family of MacDuff, and his successor, who may have been his brother, was called Gillemichael MacDuff, and from this point at least the earldom was hereditary.

That the family had royal connections may be divined from the 'Law Clan MacDuff', which is mentioned in 1384. The clan's representative had the right to place the King on the throne at his coronation; the clan should be in the front line of any battle fought by the King; and a fixed payment would secure remission from an act of murder.

William Duff of Braco, in Banffshire, who inherited the chiefship, was created Lord Braco in 1725, and Earl of Fife in the Irish peerage in 1759. Alexander W.G. Duff, 6th Earl, was made Duke of Fife in 1889 on his marriage to Princess Louise, daughter of King Edward VII.

MacEWEN

The clan was known as the MacEwens of Otter, from a mile-long sandbank which jutted out into Loch Fyne, near Kilfinan in Argyll. A Ewen of Otter is known at the beginning of the thirteenth century. Swene, last of the chiefs of Otter, gave over the lands to the Campbells in 1432, and the ownership was later confirmed to the Earl of Argyll by King James V. The MacEwens who remained became hereditary bards to Clan Campbell, and the rest, having lost their home base, scattered through Scotland, some of them acquiring the lands of Bardrochat in Ayrshire and Marchmont in Berwickshire.

MacFARLANE

The MacFarlanes are descended from the ancient earls of Lennox through Gilchrist, younger brother of Malduin, Earl of Lennox in the mid-thirteenth century, who gave him the lands of Arrochar on the west side of Loch Lomond.

The last of the former line of the earls of Lennox was executed by King James I in 1425 without there being a male heir, but instead of the title going to the chief of Clan MacFarlane, it was awarded to Sir John Stewart of Darnley, whose grandmother had been the old Earl's daughter. That the MacFarlanes did not take kindly to being overlooked is demonstrated by their opposition to the earls of Lennox, for which they lost most of their lands. The aggressive nature of the MacFarlanes was prominent also in their daily lives, and various acts had to be passed to curb their unlawful excesses, culminating in 1624 in many of them being deported to other parts of Scotland and taking different names.

MacGREGOR

The earliest clan lands of the MacGregors were in Glen Orchy, in Lorn, and after their chief had died childless, a prisoner of King Edward I of England, he was succeeded by his nephew, Gregor. A daughter of the clan married into Clan Campbell, which then included all the MacGregor territories in its policy of expansion, taking over the glens of Orchy, Strae, and Gyle, so that the landless MacGregors became known as the 'Children of the Mist'. Rob Roy MacGregor (1671-1734) was the third son of Donald Glas (*d.* 1702), 5th Chief of Glengyle.

The intricate pattern of the sword dance is further enlivened by the colourful dress of the participants. Concentration is essential, particularly for the under-nines.

MacINNES

MacInnes is from the Gaelic *aonghais* (unique choice), and members of the the clan are said to have been the original inhabitants of the region of Morven, on the mainland opposite the northwest coast of Mull, and to have been constables of Kinlochaline Castle. During the seventeenth century the lands came under the control of the Campbells, which is why in 1644 Sir Alasdair MacDonald (*d.* 1647), nicknamed *Coll Keitach* (Coll the Ambidextrous) after his father, came from Antrim, ravaged Morven, and burned the castle as a part of the overall battle plan of the Marquis of Montrose. The MacInneses now spread in all directions, and served different causes depending on where they settled.

MacINTYRE

The Gaelic *Mac-an-t-saoir* means 'son of the carpenter', the carpenter in question, according to tradition, cutting off his thumb, which he used to plug a leak in a galley. Members of the clan came from the Hebrides to Argyll, becoming foresters to the Stewarts of Lorn and then to the Campbells, from whom they leased the lands of Glen Noe for an annual payment in the summer of a white cow and a snowball (readily obtainable from the upper slopes of Ben Cruachan). The arrangement seems to have lasted until the eighteenth century, when the chief of the MacIntyres of Glenoe agreed to compound kind into cash, which finally grew to a rent of such proportions that his people had to abandon their homeland.

Duncan ban MacIntyre (1724-1812), born in Glen Orchy, was a gamekeeper who, though he never learned to write, became one of the finest, and certainly the jolliest, of all Gaelic poets.

MACKAY

In 1415 the Lord of the Isles formally granted the region of Strathnaver to Angus (*d.* 1433), Chief of Mackay, and also gave him his sister in marriage. A century later Uisdean Mackay (1561-1614) was forced to become a vassal of the Earl of Sutherland. The Barony of Farr came to the clan by charter of King James V in 1539, but in 1642 a bankrupt first lord Reay sold Strathnaver to the Sutherlands, who got the rest of the clan's territory in 1829. In the meantime General George Mackay of Scourie (1640-92) had become commander of the Crown's forces. On the general's death in action in Europe, his nephew, Aeneas Mackay (*d.* 1697), a grandson of the 1st Lord Reay, assumed command of the Mackay regiment. He married and settled in Holland, where his descendants were made barons. So it was that in 1875, on the lapse of the direct line in Scotland, Baron Eric MacKay van Ophemert succeeded as 12th Lord Reay.

MACKENZIE

It is generally accepted that the ancient earls of Ross, who held vast sway in Moray, descended from an elder son of Gilleoin of the Aird, and the Mackenzies from a younger son. Mackenzie means 'son of Kenneth', and in 1267 a Kenneth was inhabiting the strategic stronghold of Eilean Donan, at the mouth of Loch Duich, in what became the Mackenzie heartland of Kintail. From here the clan spread out to occupy territory which encompassed stretches of both the east and west coasts of the mainland. At the same time the chiefly family was multiplying. The two younger sons of Alexander (*d.* 1488), Chief of Kintail, Duncan of Hilton and Hector of Gairloch, and four grandsons, Alexander of Davochmuluag, Roderick of Achilty, Kenneth of Gilchrist, and Roderick of Redcastle, between them founded twenty-five branches of the clan, and another sixteen emerged in the seventeenth century.

Clan Mackenzie illustrates the perplexities of

loyalty. It took neither side during the campaign of the Marquis of Montrose in 1644-5, but in 1649 George (d. 1651), 2nd Earl of Seaforth, joined King Charles II in Europe, and his family fought for the King at the Battle of Worcester in 1651. The 4th and 5th earls were likewise confirmed Jacobite plotters and activists, with such disastrous results to family, lands and titles, that the clan itself had not the resources to support Bonnie Prince Charlie in 1745. George (d. 1766), 3rd Earl of Cromartie, managed to raise a small force, but it was occupied on duty elsewhere during the Battle of Culloden in April 1746. Even so, two Mackenzies were executed, 79 were transported in unbelievable conditions, and the Earl himself was condemned to death but reprieved on condition that he went to live in England. Needless to say, he lost his title, which was not revived until 1861.

MACLAREN

Maclarens held lands in Perthshire in the thirteenth century, and the MacLaurins possessed and occupied the island of Tiree from a date which may be even earlier. That the two families are connected was confirmed in 1781, when the claim of John MacLaurin (1734-96), Lord Dreghorn, judge and man of letters, to the chiefship of Clan Maclaren was established by the Lyon Court. The chiefship now resides with the Maclarens of Achleskine, who claim descent from Laurin, or Lawrence, hereditary Abbot of Achtus, Balquhidder.

Repairing Hadrian's Wall at Housestead Fort, Northumberland, which was built by the Romans to keep the Scots at bay. Unlike the English tribes, the Scots never succumbed to Roman rule.

MACLEAN OF DUART

The Macleans of Duart are chiefs of Clan Maclean. The castle and lands of Duart, on the island of Mull, were granted to them by royal charter in 1390.

One of the dynastic marriages of the clan was between Lachlan Maclean of Duart and a sister of the Earl of Argyll, but finding, or suspecting, her to be barren, in about 1520 Maclean tied her to a rock (today called Lady's Rock) in the sound between Lismore and Mull and left her to drown when the tide rose. He reported her death as being by misadventure, and travelled to Inveraray to pay his respects to her family, only to find her there, flanked by stony-faced relations. She had been rescued by a passing fishing boat.

In 1750 the Duart line became extinct when the estates were forfeited to the Campbells, but in 1912, Sir Fitzroy Maclean, 10th Baronet and 26th Chief, recovered the lands and restored the castle of Duart, re-establishing the traditional seat of the clan.

MACLEOD

Leod, son of Olaf the Black, Norse King of Man in 1230, had two sons. From Tormod (or Norman) descended the Macleods of Harris and Dunvegan, and from Torquil the Macleods of Lewis and Raasay.

At Dunvegan in Skye the Macleods built the present stronghold, which dates from the fourteenth century. It is the seat of the chief, and it houses, among other relics, the Fairy Flag, said to have been given to John, 4th Chief, by his wife, a fairy princess, but more probably a battle standard of his Norse ancestors, plundered during one of their fearsome raids in the East. Roderick (*d.* 1626), 16th Chief, known as Rory *Mór* was knighted by King James VI. He enlarged Dunvegan Castle and his estates, and established within his home an atmosphere in which poetry as well as music could flourish. Dame Flora Macleod, 28th Chief, died in 1976 at the age of 98, having travelled the world several times to visit and encourage members of her clan.

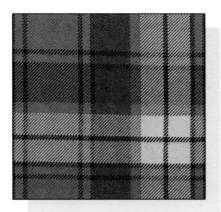

MACMILLAN

The Gaelic *MacMhaolain* means 'son of the tonsured one', which in this case would be a cleric of the ancient Celtic Church. A ringed stone cross, carved in a style of the ninth century, with a Latin inscription which reads 'This is the cross of Alexander Macmillan', still stands today in the churchyard of Kilmory Knap, Loch Sween, Argyll. The Macmillans of Knap lost the chiefship of the clan to the family of Dunmore, Loch Tarbert, in the 1660s, through whom it passed eventually to the Laggalgarve branch. Very early on, Macmillans settled in Lochaber, from where two hundred of them emigrated to Ontario, Canada, in 1802.

Kirkpatrick Macmillan (1813-78), inventor of the pedal bicycle, was a Dumfriesshire blacksmith.

The two brothers who in 1844 founded the publishing firm of Macmillan came from Arran, and share the same descent as Harold Macmillan, 1st Earl of Stockton, who was Prime Minister 1957-63.

MacNAB

Clann-an-Aba is Gaelic for 'children of the abbot', and the MacNabs are descended from the hereditary abbots of Glendochart, Loch Tay. In 1336 Gilbert MacNab received a charter of the Barony of Bovain, Glendochart, from King David II. The clan, led by 'Smooth John' MacNab, fought for the Marquis of Montrose in 1644-5, and captured the island castle of Loch Dochart.

In 1824 Archibald MacNab, 17th Chief, obtained a territorial grant of land in Ontario, Canada. Here, with several hundred MacNabs, he established MacNab as a feudal township. Before his death he made a written statement that his cousin Sir Allan MacNab (1798-1862), Prime Minister of Canada 1854-7, was representative of the line nearest to his own, which became extinct on the death of his daughter in 1894. The dormant chiefship was revived in 1955 in the person of the head of the branch of MacNab of Arthurstone.

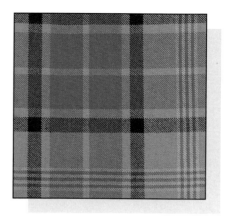

MACPHERSON

The first to bear the name was Donald Macpherson, son of Duncan, who was the Parson of Laggan in 1438. Ewen MacPherson of Cluny (*d*. 1756), Clan Chief, raised a company to fight against Bonnie Prince Charlie in 1745, and then, after the Battle of Prestonpans, brought them over to the Jacobite side. In June 1746 government soldiers burned down his mansion and all the other houses in the vicinity. He set up residence in his 'cage', a cave in the mountain face of Ben Alder, from which he emerged to give personal assistance to the Prince until his final escape, after which Macpherson lived in hiding for nine years, protected by his clansmen and tenants, before getting away to France. His estates were forfeited, but in 1784 they were returned to Ewen's son, Duncan (1750-1817), who had been born in a corn kiln during his father's period of hiding, and who became a colonel in the 3rd infantry regiment.

MAITLAND

Sir Richard of Maitland acquired the lands of Thirlestane, in the parish of Lauder, Berwickshire, through his wife, Avicia, in the thirteenth century. Lethington, in Haddington, came into the family in about 1345. Sir Richard Maitland of Lethington (1496-1586), lawyer, judge , poet, and important collector of early Scots poetry, had two notable sons. The second, John Maitland (1545-1595), judge and, from 1594, Secretary of State, was made Lord Thirlestane in 1590. His only son John (*d*. 1645), was made Earl of Lauderdale in 1624, and was President of Parliament 1644-5. His eldest son John (1616-82), Secretary of State on the Restoration of the Monarchy in 1660, was created Duke of Lauderdale in 1672, his brother Charles (1620-91) becoming 3rd Earl of Lauderdale.

The earls of Lauderdale are Hereditary Bearers of the National Flag of Scotland, an office which survives today.

MAXWELL

Maxwell, or 'Maccus's Well', is a pool of the River Tweed by Kelso. John (1553-1593), 6th Lord Maxwell, was briefly Earl of Morton after the incumbent of that title had been executed. He was killed while on an official mission to put down the Johnstons, with whom his family had a long-standing feud. His son, 7th Lord, killed Sir James Johnston in 1608 in retaliation, for which he was executed in 1613, being succeeded by his brother Robert, who was made Earl of Nithsdale in about 1620. William (*d*. 1744), 5th Earl, was sentenced to death for his part in the Rebellion of 1715. The day before his execution he was visited several times in the Tower of London by his wife, always accompanied by one or more female companions. The guards, confused by all these comings and goings, failed to notice that the figure who left with the Countess towards dusk was the Earl himself, dressed in female clothing.

MacRAE

MacRath in Gaelic means 'son of grace', and it is a personal name which first appears in Scottish records in the twelfth century.

The family known as MacRae is said to have originated in the territory of the Frasers of Lovat, on the Beauly Firth. Three sons left home at the beginning of the fourteenth century, and founded dynasties at Brahan (near Dingwall), in Argyll, and in Kintail, where they became bodyguards to the chief of the Mackenzies of Kintail.

Duncan MacRae, 5th Chief of Kintail, was granted the lands of Inverinate in about 1557. The MacRaes of Conchra are descended from Rev. John MacRae (1614-1673) of Dingwall. Many MacRaes left Kintail in the wake of the clearances in the early years of the nineteenth century, to settle in Nova Scotia. After the potato famines of 1846-7, of a boatload of a hundred emigrants going to join a ship for Montreal, fifty were called MacRae.

MUIR

The name means 'living by a moor or heath', and in 1291 Thomas de la More was executor of the will of Divorgilla, mother of King John (Balliol). The future King Robert II married Elizabeth, daughter of Sir Adam Mure of Rowallan, in 1346. Later the marriage was challenged, possibly on the grounds of there being a degree of consanguinity between them, and a dispensation from the Pope was granted in 1347, when the legitimacy of their children, including the future King Robert III, was accepted.

Alexander Muir Mackenzie (1764-1835), created a baronet in 1805, was of the line of Muirs of Cassencarie, and took his additional name on inheriting his uncle's estates in Perthshire. John Muir of Deanston (1828-1903), Provost of Glasgow, who was made a baronet in 1892, was the son of John Muir (1736-1851), a Glasgow merchant. Edwin Muir (1887-1959), poet and critic, was born in Deerness, Orkney, the son of a farmer.

MURRAY

The ultimate ancestor of all the Murrays is said to be Freskin, a Pict or possibly a Fleming, who was given charge of part of Moray by King David I in the twelfth century. His grandson William (d. 1226) called himself 'de Moravia', and from one of his sons descended the Murrays of Tullibardine. Sir John Murray, 12th Laird, was created Earl of Tullibardine by King James VI in 1606.

By a marriage with the heiress of the Stewart earls of Atholl, the Murrays of Tullibardine became marquises and then, in 1703, dukes of Atholl. It was the Marquis of Tullibardine who unfurled the royal standard to introduce Bonnie Prince Charlie to his troops at Glenfinnan in 1745, and his brother Lord George Murray (1694-1760) was one of the Prince's generals in the campaign, during which he laid siege to the family seat, Blair Castle, Perthshire, which was occupied by government troops.

The 10th Duke of Atholl (*b.* 1931) lives in the

castle, part of which dates from 1269, and is Clan Chief, besides being the only British subject who has the right to maintain a private army, the Atholl Highlanders.

Sheep-farming has become a way of life for many in Scotland since the eighteenth century, though the work is hard and the living certainly not easy.

NAIRN(E)

Nairn is the burgh in Moray, the first person of that name to be recorded being Adam de Narryn, chaplain of the altar of the Blessed Virgin at Inverness. Robert Nairne (*d*. 1652), of Mukkersy, Perthshire, President of the Court of Session, was the father of Robert Nairne (*d*. 1683) who was appointed a judge at the Restoration of the Monarchy, and created Lord Nairne in 1681. He was succeeded in the title by his son-in-law, Lord William Murray (*d*. 1726), who was convicted of treason after the 1715 Rebellion and condemned to death, but was reprieved and merely attainted. His eldest son John (*d*. 1770) was also attainted and was attainted again after the '45 Rebellion. The title was restored to his grandson, William Nairne (1757-1830), who became 5th Lord Nairne.

Michael Nairn (1804-58), of Kirkcaldy, founded the Scottish linoleum industry. His son, Michael Nairn (1838-1915), was created a baronet in 1904.

NAPIER

'Napery' is linen, and the naperer was in charge of the royal linen. John de Napier held lands in Dunbartonshire in the thirteenth century. His descendant Alexander Napier, Provost of Edinburgh in 1437, made such a fortune as a wool-merchant that he was able to lend money to King James I, against the security of the lands of Merchiston, which were never redeemed. John Napier (1550-1617), 8th Laird, invented the first calculating-machine (known as 'Napier's Bones'), as well as an armoured tank and a submarine.

Descendants of the Merchiston branch have been notable soldiers, including General Sir Charles Napier (1782-1853), conqueror of Sind, and his brother General Sir William Napier (1785-1860), who served in the Peninsular War. Their cousin, Admiral Sir Charles Napier (1786-1860), served and fought in many naval sectors, including North America, and commanded the Baltic Fleet in 1854.

OGILVY

Gilbert, third son of Gillebride, Earl of Angus, was granted a charter of the Barony of Ogilvy in about 1172. His descendant, Sir Walter Ogilvy of Lintrathan (*d*. 1440), Lord High Treasurer of Scotland, founded the line of Airlie. His grandson, Sir James, was created Lord Ogilvy of Airlie by King James IV in 1491. James (1593-1666), 8th Lord Airlie, was made Earl of Airlie by King Charles I in 1639. It was his castle, 'The Bonnie House of Airlie' in the ballad of that name, which was wrecked by the Marquis of Argyll and his Covenanters in 1640. In 1645, after the Battle of Philiphaugh, his son James (1615-1704), 2nd Earl, was captured and imprisoned for the second time for his support of the Marquis of Montrose. He was tried and sentenced to death, but the day before his execution he changed places with his elder sister, who was visiting him, and escaped from St Andrews Castle wearing her clothes. David (1725-1803), Lord Ogilvy, son of the 4th Earl, joined Bonnie Prince Charlie. Afterwards he escaped to France, and was later pardoned in the light of his youth, though the earldom was not restored to the family until 1826. In 1963 Hon. (now Sir) Angus Ogilvy (*b*. 1928), second son of the 12th Earl of Airlie, married Princess Alexandra of Kent, first cousin of Her Majesty the Queen.

A peat cutter rests from his labours in the spring sunshine.

PORTEOUS

The origin of the name is obscure, but it was entrenched in Peebleshire and Fife in the fifteenth century. John Porteous, Captain of the Edinburgh City Guard, ordered his men to fire on a mob which was demonstrating at the execution of a smuggler in 1736, killing several people. He was convicted of murder and sentenced to death, but reprieved. He was then seized from prison by a body of men, who hanged him from the pole outside a dyer's shop.

Dr William Porteous (1735-1812), Minister of the Wynd Church, Glasgow, was so orthodox in his views that he rigorously opposed the use of the organ in church, but was also rational and brave enough to preach a sermon on 'Toleration' in November 1778, at the height of the mob violence which followed the repeal of acts penalising Roman Catholics, and which was condoned by other churchmen and most of the Scottish synods.

RAMSAY

Simon de Ramsay, of Anglo-Norman descent, lived in Lothian in the twelfth century. William Ramsay of Dalhousie swore homage to King Edward I of England in 1296 but then joined the forces of King Robert I (the Bruce). His son, Sir Alexander Ramsay (*d.* 1342), was an even greater thorn in the English side, raising the siege of Dunbar Castle in 1342 by running in provisions by boat, and capturing Roxburgh Castle in 1342, for which he was made Governor of the castle and Sheriff of Teviotdale by King David II. Unfortunately William Douglas (1300-53), Knight of Liddesdale, who had held both posts earlier, was so incensed that he kidnapped Ramsay and starved him to death.

Allan Ramsay (1684-1758), master wig maker, founder of the first British circulating library, poet, and dramatist, was descended from the Ramsays of Cockpen. His son Allan (1713-84) was royal portrait painter to King George III.

ROBERTSON

Duncan 'the Stout', founder and 1st Chief of Clan Donnachaidh, was descended from the ancient earls of Atholl and through them from Crinan, Abbot of Dunkeld, who was also father of King Duncan I. Duncan 'the Stout' led his clan at the Battle of Bannockburn in 1314, on the way to which the tip of the battle standard is said mysteriously to have acquired, during the night, the piece of rock crystal

Even today, much of the Highlands is bleak and the living can be harsh.

which has been the clan's talisman ever since. Robert 'the Grizzled', 4th Chief, from whom the clan took its name of Robertson, hunted down and captured in a lonely Atholl glen the murderers of King James I, and handed them over to a grisly justice. When King James II came of age, he rewarded Robert by creating his lands in Atholl the Barony of Struan.

Alexander Robertson (1670-1749), 13th Chief, known as the 'Poet Chief', was studying for the Church at St Andrews University when he suddenly became chief on the deaths of his father and elder brother. In 1689 he left university to take up arms for Viscount Dundee, against the wishes of his

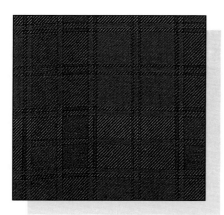

formidable mother, who wrote round to the clan branches: 'He is going to Badenoch just now; for Christ's sake come in all haste and stop him, for he will not be advised by me.' They delayed him only long enough to catch up with him with their men. Alexander was 'out' in 1715, too, and again in 1745. Having personally led the clan at the Battle of Prestonpans, he was persuaded to return home, which he did in style in the captured coach of the defeated general, though he had to be carried, carriage and all, the last part of the way, the road not being suitable for wheels.

In March 1746, when Lord George Murray besieged Blair Castle, which was occupied by Hanoverian troops, the first cannon was fired by Lady Robertson of Lude, who had acted as hostess the previous year when Bonnie Prince Charlie had visited the castle. There is a Clan Donnachaidh Museum at Bruar, four miles from Blair Atholl.

ROSE

Hugh Rose of Geddes, Invernessshire, whose ancestor may have come to England after the Norman Conquest with Bishop Odo of Bayeux, witnessed the charter of foundation of Beauly Priory in 1219. His son, Hugh, acquired by marriage the lands of Kilravock, Nairn, on which another Hugh Rose, 7th Laird of Kilravock, built the old castle tower in 1460. Both lands and castle are still in the family.

Though the clan supported the Government in 1689, 1715, and 1745, the 16th Laird agreed to entertain Bonnie Prince Charlie at the castle just before the Battle of Culloden in 1746.

Field-Marshal Hugh Rose (1801-85) volunteered for service during the Indian Mutiny, and between 1857 and 1860, as commander-in-chief, he won numerous battles and recaptured many forts and several towns. He was made Lord Strathnairn in 1866.

ROSS

Ross means 'promontory', and the first of the ancient earls of Ross was Ferquhard Macintaggart, who was rewarded with the title by King Alexander II in 1215. The chiefship remained with the Balnagown branch until the death of the 13th Laird in 1711, when the estate was settled on the Rosses of Hawkhead, represented by William (1656-1738), 12th Lord Ross and descendant of Sir John Ross of Hawkhead, one of the three Scottish champions chosen to joust against three French knights before King James II in 1449. This family, however, could not claim any connection with the original earls of Ross, and the direct line continued through the Rosses of Pitcalnie, descended from a son of the 10th Laird of Balnagown, who re-established the right to the chiefship in 1903. In 1936 it passed to the family of Ross of Shandwick, Nigg, whose most notable member is Sir Ronald Ross (1857-1931), discoverer of the cause of malaria.

RUTHVEN

The ruins of Ruthven Barracks, Perthshire, stand in the lands granted to the family in about 1298. Sir William Ruthven was made Lord Ruthven in 1487. Patrick (1520-66), 3rd Lord Ruthven, rose from his sickbed to lead the murderers of David Rizzio, favourite of Mary, Queen of Scots, into her private chamber in 1566.

John (1578-1600), 3rd Earl, was killed in his house in Perth in a mix-up known as the 'Gowrie Conspiracy' – an alleged attempt to murder the King. The earldom was abolished and the name of Ruthven proscribed until 1641. Thomas Ruthven of Freeland, descended from the 2nd Lord Ruthven, was created Lord Ruthven in 1651. His descendant, Walter, 8th Lord Ruthven of Freeland, was created 1st Lord Ruthven in the United Kingdom peerage in 1919. His son, Alexander Hore-Ruthven (1872-1955), a Governor-General of Australia, was made 1st Earl of Gowrie of the new creation in 1945.

SCOTT

Uchtredus filius Scotus, 'Uchtred, son of the Scot', witnessed charters between 1107 and 1128. From his two sons descended the Scotts of Balweary (Fife) and the Scotts of Buccleuch (Selkirk). Sir Walter Scott of Buccleuch (1565-1611) was created Lord Scott in 1606, and his son Walter was made Earl of Buccleuch in 1619. Anne, Countess of Buccleuch, to whom the earldom and the chiefship of the clan passed after the deaths of her father, 2nd Earl, in 1651 and subsequently of her elder sister, married James, Duke of Monmouth (1649-1685), when they were made Duke and Duchess of Buccleuch.

Walter Scott of Harden (*d.* 1629) was a great cattle-rustler. From him descended Sir Walter Scott (1771-1832), 1st Laird of Abbotsford, poet, novelist and instigator of much of the tartan image. The direct line of descent of his baronetcy continued through his daughter Sophia (*d.* 1837).

SCRYMGEOUR

Alexander Schyrmeschur was in 1298 confirmed as Royal Standard Bearer, a hereditary office first held by Sir Alexander Carron (nicknamed 'Skirmisher') in the reign of King Alexander I and still held by the family's representative today. He was also made Constable of Dundee, near which he was granted lands. The lands of Glassary, Argyll, came to the family in the fourteenth century.

John Scrymgeour (*d.* 1643) was created Viscount Dudhope in 1641. John (*d.* 1668), 3rd Viscount, was made Earl of Dundee in 1660 for his loyal and active support of King Charles II. His son, John Scrymgeour (*d.* 1698) was deprived of the titles by John Maitland (1616-82), 1st Duke of Lauderdale, who gave Dudhope Castle to his brother. On the brother's conviction for mismanaging the Mint, the castle was forfeited in 1683 and given by Charles II to Viscount Dundee, a relative of the Scrymgeour family. The titles were restored in 1953.

SETON

Seton means 'sea town', and probably referred originally to Tranent, a few miles east of Edinburgh, where Alexander Seton held lands in about 1150. Sir Christopher Seton (1278-1306) was hanged by the English for his support of King Robert I (the Bruce), his brother-in-law. Sir Alexander Seton, probably his brother, was Governor of Berwick from 1327 to 1333, when it was surrendered to the English after they had hanged his son who had been given as a hostage. His heiress, Margaret, married Alan of Winton in about 1347, and from them descended the lords Seton.

George (1530-85), 5th Lord Seton, supported Mary, Queen of Scots after the murders of David Rizzio in 1566 and her husband, Lord Darnley, in 1567, and aided her escape from Lochleven Castle in 1568. His second son, Robert (*d*. 1607), 6th Lord, was created Earl of Winton by her son, King James VI, in 1600.

SKENE

It is said that in the eleventh century a son of the chief of Clan Donnachaidh (Robertson) saved his king by killing a wolf with his *sgian* (dagger), for which he was rewarded with the lands of Skene, Aberdeenshire. The estate passed to the earls of Fife by inheritance when the original family line failed in 1827. John Skene of Curriehill (1543-1617) was created Lord Curriehill on his appointment as a judge of the Court of Session in 1594. His first son, Sir James Skene (*d*. 1633)was created a baronet of Nova Scotia in 1630, while his second son was John Skene of Hallyards, Fife, who became Lord Clerk Register. It was one of the Skenes of Hallyards who founded Skeneborough on Lake Champlain in North America.

A notable member of the Skenes of Rubislaw, Aberdeenshire, was Dr William Forbes Skene (1809-92), Historiographer Royal for Scotland and author of *Celtic Scotland*.

SMITH

Smith means 'worker in iron', and the name first occurs in southeast Scotland in the thirteenth century. The most notable family of the name emerged in the Barony of Mugdock, in the parish of Strathblane, Stirlingshire, where for four hundred years its members were hereditary tenants of Craigend and armourers, latterly to the Grahams of Montrose. Adam Smith (1723-90), the political economist, was born in Kirkcaldy, though his father came from Aberdeen. James Smith (1789-1850), inventor of the thorough drainage system of agriculture, was born in Glasgow of parents from Galloway. William Robertson Smith (1846-94), scholar and theologian, was born in Keig, Aberdeenshire. Sydney Goodsir Smith (1915-75), foremost of the second wave of poets of the Scottish Renaissance, was born in New Zealand. Iain Crichton Smith (b. 1928), poet and novelist, who writes also in Gaelic, was born in the island of Lewis.

STEWART

The line of Stewart monarchs of Scotland, and then of Great Britain, which lasted from 1371 to 1714, descended from Marjorie, daughter of King Robert I (the Bruce), and her husband Walter, 6th High Steward (or Stewart) of Scotland, who at the age of 21 had commanded the centre of the Scottish army at the Battle of Bannockburn in 1314. His ancestor, and 1st High Steward, which was a hereditary office from 1157, was Walter Fitz Alan, the younger son of the Sheriff of Shropshire. Alexander, 4th High Steward's second son, Sir John Stewart of Bonkyl (or Buncle or Bonkhill, meaning 'the church at the foot of the hill'), Berwickshire, was the ancestor of numerous notable branches of the name, including the earls of Galloway, the Stewart earls of Atholl, and the Stewarts of Appin. From one of King Robert II's illegitimate sons descended the marquises of Bute, and from illegitimate sons of his legitimate fourth son, Alexander (1343-1405), Earl of Buchan,

A baronial mansion at Inveran, Easter Ross. The Victorians were great admirers of medieval architecture.

'Wolf of Badenoch', many families of the name of Stewart in Aberdeenshire, Atholl, Banffshire, and Moray.

If the tartan known as Prince Charles Edward really was, as it is claimed, worn by Bonnie Prince Charlie and his followers in 1745, then this would be the earliest form in which the Royal Stewart tartan appeared. In which case, of almost as early an origin would be the sett of the Stewart of Fingask tartan, which is said to derive from a cloak left by him at Fingask Castle near Perth in 1746. The Royal Stewart tartan is not a clan tartan, but the property of the Royal Family.

57

TENNANT

The name is first recorded in 1309. John Tennant of Glenconner (1726-1810), whose ancestors were tenant farmers near Ayr in the fifteenth century, was a friend of the poet Robert Burns (1759-96), who wrote a verse epistle to his son, in which several other members of the family are referred to. His great-grandson Charles Tennant (1823-1906) was created a baronet in 1885. His eldest son, Sir Edward Tennant (1859-1920), Lord Lieutenant of Peebles 1908-20, was made 1st Lord Glenconner in 1911.

A family by the name of Tennent was established as farmers and private brewers at Easter Common, Glasgow, in 1556. A descendant built the Saracen's Head Inn, whose comforts, and coal fire, Dr Johnson and James Boswell enjoyed in 1773, while three years later John and Robert Tennent founded the public brewery which still bears their names.

THOM(P)SON

'Son of Thomas' is a common appellation throughout Scotland. There is a Thomson sept of Clan Campbell, and also one of MacThomas. Derick Thomson (*b.* 1921), born on the island of Lewis, has been Professor of Celtic at Glasgow University since 1963, and is a distinguished modern poet both in English and, as Ruaraidh MacThómais, in Gaelic. Alexander Thomson (1460-1513), said to have been the grandson of a bastard son of the 11th Earl of Mar, grandson of King Robert II, was born in Corstorphine, near Edinburgh, and died at the Battle of Flodden. His descendants are described as being 'of Corstorphine'. Frederick Thomson (1875-1935), Solicitor-General for Scotland 1923-4, who was created a baronet in 1929, was the grandson of a native of Linlithgow. He was succeeded by his son, Sir Douglas Thomson (1905-72), of Glendarroch, Midlothian.

WALLACE

Wallensis, in Latin, meant a Briton of Strathclyde, which was a separate kingdom until 1018. In about 1170 Richard Wallensis obtained the lands of Riccarton in Ayrshire. His grandson, Adam, had two sons, of whom the younger was Sir Malcom Wallace of Elderslie, Renfrewshire, father of Sir William Wallace (1274-1305), the national hero. Sir William was not only a patriot and fearsome warrior, but a great leader, who established a chain of military command much like that in the army today, and who defeated the English at the Battle of Stirling Bridge in 1297, pushing them out of Scotland altogether for a time. He was finally betrayed, captured, and taken in chains to London. There he was tried for treason, which he could hardly be regarded as having committed, in that he had not signed the oath of allegiance to King Edward I. Nevertheless he was convicted, and sentenced to be hanged, drawn and quartered.

WATSON

Watson, 'son of Walter', first occurs as a name in Edinburgh in 1392. Robert Watson (1746-1838), who was born in Elgin, claimed to have fought on the American side in the War of Independence of 1775-8. After his return to Britain he led a lively life, avoiding arrest by escaping to France, from where he moved to Rome, always hoping that his money-making schemes, which included the purchase for £22. 10s of two cartloads of Jacobite archives, would bring him riches rather than notoriety. He finally strangled himself in a London tavern. By contrast, George Watson (1767-1837), who was born on his father's estate in Berwickshire, was a distinguished portrait painter who became first President of the Royal Scottish Academy.

WEIR

The name derives from the Norman place-name Vere. Ralph de Ver, from whom the Weirs of Blackwood, Lanarkshire, claim descent, was captured, with King William I (the Lion), in 1174 while besieging the castle of Alnwick in Northumberland. Others of the name held lands in Lesmahagow, Lanarkshire, in the fifteenth century.

Major Thomas Weir (1599-1670), born at Kirkton House, Carluke, was burned at the stake in Edinburgh for incest, adultery, bestiality, and witchcraft, his sister being hanged the next day for her part in some of his activities. Subsequently, his ghost was said to have been seen galloping down the High Street on a headless black horse.

William Weir (1877-1950), engineer, industrialist, and statesman, who was descended from an illegitimate daughter of the poet Robert Burns(1759-96), was created 1st Viscount Weir in 1918.

WILSON

The name means 'son of Will' and is first recorded in Scotland at the beginning of the fifteenth century. James Wilson, whose father was from Eastforth, Lanark, bought the lands of Hinschelwood and Cleugh, Carnwath, in 1655. His descendant John Wilson (1809-89), of Airdrie, was created a baronet in 1906. David Wilson (1805-98), of Carbeth, who was descended from a family which lived in Berwickshire in the seventeenth century, was made a baronet in 1920. Another notable family is that of Wilson of Ashmore, Perthshire, whose ancestor was James Wilson (1829-1905), solicitor, of Falkirk. Wilsons of Bannockburn were pioneers in the industrialisation of tartan weaving and in the marketing of clan and district tartans.